SEASON *of* WONDERS

Celebrating the Miracle of Christmas

By JOSEPH M. MARTIN
Narration by PAMELA MARTIN
Orchestration by BRANT ADAMS & STAN PETHEL

Pg.4..CAROLS .... 'G
Pg.20..............COME, THOU LONG-EXPE.........US
Pg.31........BETHLEHEM PROMISE, BETHLEH.. JOY
Pg.44................................REJOICE, ALL YE DAUGHTERS
Pg.56..ALL ON A STARRY NIGHT
Pg.61..GLORY AND WONDER
Pg.70..............SAW YOU NEVER, IN THE TWILIGHT
Pg.79................................THE WONDER OF CHRISTMAS
Pg.89..O HOLY NIGHT

Performance Time: Approx. 45 minutes

Harold Flammer
M U S I C

A Division of Shawnee Press, Inc.
1221 17th Avenue South • Nashville, TN 37212

Visit Shawnee Press Online at www.shawneepress.com

FOREWORD

When we ponder the miracles surrounding the birth of Jesus, we discover in abundance the lavish character of God's love. Soaring above our human understanding is an amazing grace that unexpectedly wraps divinity in swaddling clothes. Beyond our dreams we find an artful mercy that decorates the dust of a rustic stable with everlasting light. We encounter the glory of God pouring over the walls of heaven and filling the darkness with angel choirs and dancing stars. We stand amazed at the mystery and majesty of God's awesome power and His infinite tenderness. Perhaps most amazing of all are the myriad ways in which celebrating these marvels of old awaken in us today a sense of the divine and fill us with a child-like wonder. In the singing of this work, may you draw close to the manger and open your heart to the unexpected glories of this season of wonders.

JOSEPH M. MARTIN

PERFORMANCE NOTES

The word "angel" comes from the Greek word "angelos" which means "messenger." The Hebrew word for "angel" is "malak," also meaning "messenger." In the Bible, the word "angel" or "messenger" often applies to heavenly beings, but occasionally is used to represent human messengers. These angels, or messengers, perform many tasks – heralding events, providing guidance, sharing news, providing warnings, protecting, announcing signs and wonders – all in service of God.

Many of the signs and wonders throughout the Bible were announced by God's messengers, and we ourselves are instructed to be messengers in Acts 1:8 (". . . and you will be my witnesses in Jerusalem, and in Samaria, and to the ends of the earth.")

In performing this work, different "messengers" announce the various narrations. Be creative in determining how these narrators dress, whether they read from a scroll or carry a candle, as well as their placement in the sanctuary. (The messenger who announces to the shepherds could announce from the balcony or the choir loft. The messenger of witness could stand among the congregation. The messenger to the world could stand in the pulpit.) Use spotlights where possible to draw attention to the narrators, and make certain that they can be heard, using microphones if needed.

Miracles and wonders are meant to be shared. Their purpose is to reveal a larger truth, to glorify the One from whom such power comes. The events surrounding the birth of Christ are a series of wonders: from ancient prophecy, celestial phenomena (the star and the angels), and historical mandates (the census), to physical miracles (the virgin birth). In this season of wonders, may we add our voices to those of prophets and angels as servant messengers of God.

Carols of Gathering

Words by
Gerhard Tersteegen (1697-1769)
John Francis Wade (1711-1786)
  tr. Frederick Oakeley (1802-1880) *and others*
Johann A. Schulz (1747-1800), *alt.*

Incorporating tunes:
WUNDERBARER KÖNIG,
ADESTE FIDELES *and* **SCHULZ**
Arranged by
JOSEPH M. MARTIN (BMI)

* Tune: WUNDERBARER KÖNIG, Joachim Neander (1650-1680)
  Words: Gerhard Tersteegen (1697-1769)

si - lence, and be - fore Him bow with rev - 'rence.

Him a - lone, God we own.

To our Lord__ and Sav - ior prais - es sing__ for-

ev - er. prais - es sing___ for - ev -

Flowing steadily ($\bullet$ = ca. 104) ③

er.___ *mf unis.* *O

Flowing steadily ($\bullet$ = ca. 104) l.h.

come, all ye faith - ful, joy - ful and tri -

* Tune: ADESTE FIDELES, John Francis Wade (1711-1786)
Words: John Francis Wade (1711-1786); tr. Frederick Oakeley (1802-1880) and others

* Tune: SCHULZ, Johann A. Schulz (1747-1800)
Words: Johann A. Schulz, *alt*.

dore Him,___ Christ_____ the Lord! Al - le -

dore___ Him,___ Christ_____ the Lord! Al - le -

lu - ia! Al - le - lu - ia! Christ is born!_____

lu - ia! Al - le - lu - ia! Christ is born!_____

THE MESSENGER OF THE ANCIENTS

And it came to pass that the people said in their hearts, "If the Lord is with us, where are all His wonders that our fathers told us about? We have been given no miraculous signs; no prophets are left, and none of us knows how long we must wait. O Lord, our souls yearn for You in the night; our spirits long for You in the morning. We wait for You, for You are the desire of our hearts."

Come, Thou Long-Expected Jesus

Incorporating tunes:
HYFRYDOL
AUSTRIAN HYMN
Arranged by
JOSEPH M. MARTIN (BMI)

Words by
CHARLES WESLEY (1707-1788)

* Tune: HYFRYDOL, Rowland H. Prichard (1811-1887)

Is - ra el's strength____ and con - so -

la - tion, hope of all____ the earth___ Thou art;____

dear___ de - sire___ of ev - 'ry na - tion,

joy of ev - 'ry long - ing

heart.___

* Tune: AUSTRIAN HYMN, Franz Joseph Haydn (1732-1809)

Come, Thou long - ex - pect - ed Je - sus. God with us! Come, Em - man - u - el!

THE MESSENGER OF PROMISE

Then the Lord said, "Before you, I will do wonders never before done in any nation in all the world. And you, Bethlehem, in the land of Judah, are by no means the least; for out of you will come a ruler who will be the shepherd of my people Israel."

Bethlehem Promise, Bethlehem Joy

Words and music by
JOSEPH M. MARTIN (BMI)
Incorporating an
Ancient Hebrew Folk Song
and **NOEL NOUVELET**

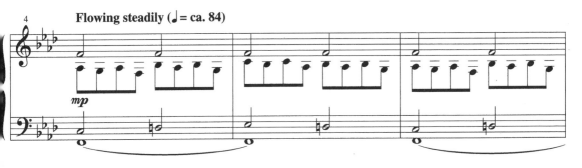

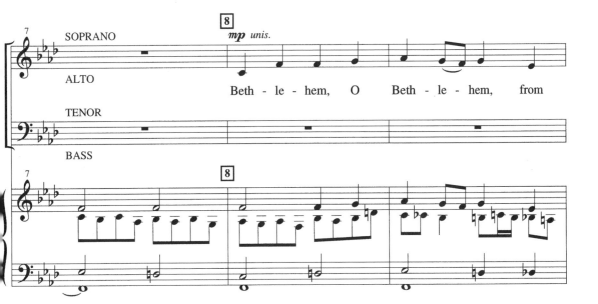

man - u - el. Ve - ni, ve - ni.

Come, Em - man - u - el.

rit.

46 Quickly, joyfull dancing (♩= ca. 120)

46 Quickly, joyfull dancing (♩= ca. 120)

rit.

mf

f

* Tune: Hebrew Folk Song

38

* Tune: NOEL NOUVELET, Traditional French Carol

Sing we all ho-san - na, Sing we___ all no - el.

Sing we no - el!

Re - joice all Is - ra - el!

Sing we all ho - san - na. Sing we___ all no -

Sing with ju - bi - la - tion! Sing out in ex - pec - ta - tion!

unis.

Sing we no - el! Re -

Sing to ev - 'ry na - tion! Sing al - le - lu - ia!

joice all Is - ra - el!

unis.

Un - to us a Son is__ giv - en. To us, a child is born.

Sing we all ho - san - na!

THE MESSENGER OF FAVOR

And in the sixth month, the angel Gabriel appeared to a virgin named Mary. And he said to her, "Do not be afraid, for you have found favor with God and will give birth to a son. The Lord God will give Him the throne of his father David and His kingdom will never end." Then Mary glorified the Lord and rejoiced. For the prophet Isaiah had foretold these things: "A virgin will be with child and will give birth to a son." Therefore, daughters of Zion, rejoice! Your King is coming, the holy One, the Savior of the world.

Rejoice, All Ye Daughters

Tune: **SANS DAY CAROL**
Traditional English Carol
Arranged by
JOSEPH M. MARTIN (BMI)

Words by
JOSEPH M. MARTIN

* Go to the "ng" immediately.

Ev - 'ry val - ley be__ lift - ed; each moun - tain made low.__ The__ crook - ed and__

glo - ry of the Lord___ shall shine like the sun; and the

eyes of the___ na - tions shall see it as one.___

For a

THE MESSENGER OF SALVATION

And Mary went to Bethlehem with Joseph, to whom she was pledged to be married. While they were there, she gave birth to her firstborn, a son. And she wrapped Him in cloth and placed Him in a manger, because there was no room for them in the inn.

There were shepherds living in the fields nearby, watching their flocks under the starry skies of night. An angel of the Lord appeared and told them, "I bring good news of great joy. This day a Savior has been born, who is Christ the Lord. This will be a sign to you: You will find a baby wrapped in cloths and lying in a manger."

All on a Starry Night

Words by
J. PAUL WILLIAMS (ASCAP)

Music by
JOSEPH GRAHAM (BMI)
and JOSEPH M. MARTIN (BMI)

* Accompanist may play voice parts if necessary.

Shep-herds heard the mu - sic from a - bove,

mu - sic sound-ing from a - bove,

fall-ing__ like__ a gen-tle snow, fill-ing all the

earth with songs of love.__ Long a - go on a

touch the__ earth,

star - ry night,__ Love__ came__ down__ to__ touch the earth,

bless-ing all with__ ho - ly__ light__ at the Sav-ior's birth.__

Underneath a cloud-less sky, an-gels sing a
lul-la-by,___ words of___ peace___ to___ hu-man-kind___
all on a star-ry night,___ all on a star-ry night.___
*Si - ent night,___ ho - ly night,___
all on a star-ry night.___

* Tune: STILLE NACHT, Franz Gruber (1787-1863)
  Words: Joseph Mohr (1792-1848)

THE MESSENGERS OF PRAISE

The shepherds said to one another, "Let us go to Bethlehem and see this thing that has happened." And they hurried and found Mary and Joseph, and the baby lying in a manger. When they had seen Him, the shepherds returned, glorifying God for all that they had heard and seen. And all who heard of it were amazed by what the shepherds told them.

Glory and Wonder

Tune: **McCRAY**
Traditional Polish Carol
Arranged by
JOSEPH M. MARTIN (BMI)

Words by
JOSEPH M. MARTIN

Je - sus Christ is born_____ to - day.

Come, see the an - gels

wing - ing through heav - en. Lis - ten to them sing - ing.

Come, see the an - gels. Lis - ten to them sing - ing._____

Raise ev - 'ry voice in songs of ad - o - ra - tion.

Sing ev - 'ry na - tion. Sing all cre - a - tion. From ev - 'ry moun - tain,

ring ju - bi - la - tion. Glo - ry, al - le - lu - ia! Glo - ry, al - le - lu - ia!

Je - sus Christ is born____ to - day.____

Je - sus Christ is born to -

day,_____ to - day!

THE MESSENGERS OF JOY

After Jesus was born in Bethlehem, Magi from the east came to Jerusalem and asked, "Where is the one who has been born king of the Jews? For we saw His star in the east and have come to worship Him." And the star went ahead of them until it came to rest over the place where the child was. And when they saw it, they were overjoyed. They bowed down before the child and worshiped Him. Then they opened their treasures and presented Him with gifts of gold, incense and myrrh. And all this was to fulfill the words of the prophet: "I who created the stars in the heavens and stretched them out, I will make you a light for the Gentiles. Nations will come to your light and kings to the brightness of your dawn."

Saw You Never, in the Twilight

Music by
JOSEPH M. MARTIN (BMI)
Incorporating tune:
GREENSLEEVES

Words by
CECIL FRANCES ALEXANDER (1823-1895) *alt.*

SOPRANO / ALTO *or* TENOR / BASS *or* MALE SOLO

Saw you

nev - er, in the twi - light, when the sun had left the

skies, up in heav'n the clear stars shin - ing through the

gloom, like sil - ver eyes? So of old the wise men,

watch - ing, saw a lit - tle strang - er star, and they

knew the King was giv - en, and they fol - lowed

* Tune: GREENSLEEVES, Traditional English Tune
  Words: Joseph M. Martin

Come, come and wor - ship Him, the

Babe, the Son of Ma - ry.

with confidence
unis.

Know you not that low - ly Ba - by was the

bring: love and faith   and   true de - vo - tion   for our

Sav - ior,   God   and   King!

Christ our   King!   Christ our   King!

THE MESSENGERS OF WITNESS

Look to the Lord and seek His face. Remember His wonders and the miracles He has done. Declare His glory among the nations, His wonders among all people. For He has caused the blind to see and the deaf to hear, the lame to dance and the silent to sing for joy. He has released the prisoners from darkness into light, and He has comforted the grieving and turned their sadness into joy. For God is able to meet all our needs through Jesus Christ. Come, let us bow down in worship, let us kneel before the Lord our Maker, for He is our God.

The Wonder of Christmas

Words and music by
JOSEPH M. MARTIN (BMI)
Incorporating tune:
ADESTE FIDELES

Slowly, with expression (♩ = ca. 88)

ACCOMP.

SOLO (optional S.A. unison)

Come, all ye faith - ful and kneel at the man - ger.

Come, find a treas - ure more cost - ly than gold.

SOLO (optional S.A. unison)

Come, know the won - der of Christ - mas.

All who are wea - ry, all who are search - ing,

treas - ure. Come to the won - der a lit - tle child will

lead,_____ a lit - tle child will lead._____

Come, learn the song that is wor - thy of

an - gels. Come, share the mes - sage that chang - es the world. Come, feel the spir - it that o - pens the heav - ens.

With great freedom and expression (♩ = ca. 84)

*O come, let us a - dore___ Him. O come, let us a -

A -

dore___ Him. O come, let us a - dore__ Him,__ Christ___ the

dore Him.

slowing to the end

(stagger breathing)

Lord. Christ the Lord. Christ the Lord!____

(stagger breathing)

slowing to the end

* Words and tune ADESTE FIDELES, John F. Wade (1711-1786)

THE MESSENGERS TO THE WORLD

There is a time for everything and a season for every purpose under heaven. The Lord said, "Unless you saw miraculous signs and wonders, you would not believe. Therefore, I have astounded my people with wonder upon wonders." This is the season of wonders. Give thanks to the Lord; tell the nations what He has done. How great are His signs, and how mighty His wonders!

dedicated to my mother-in-law, Cleva Collar, and her family
in celebration of the life of Robert Jay Collar who loved to sing

O Holy Night

Tune: **CANTIQUE NOEL**
by ALDOLPHE ADAM (1803-1856)
Arranged by

Words by
JOHN S. DWIGHT (1813-1893)

JOSEPH M. MARTIN (BMI)

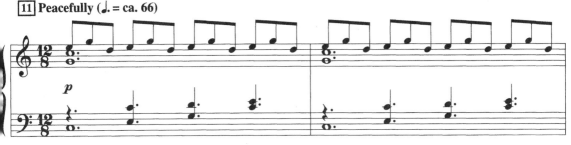

shin - ing. It is the night of the dear Sav - ior's

birth._____ Long lay the world_____ in

sin and er - ror pin - ing, till He ap -

peared and the soul felt its worth._____ A

thrill of hope, the wea - ry world re - joic - es, for

yon - der breaks a new and glo - rious morn.

(end solo)

Fall_____ on your knees. O

love one an - oth - er. His law is

love and His gos - pel is peace.

God is our friend,_____ for Christ is now our

broth - er, and in His name all op - pres - sion shall

cease. Sweet hymns of joy in

grate - ful cho - rus raise we. Let all with - in us

praise His ho - ly name. Christ_____ is the

Lord!_____ O praise_____ His name for -

ev - er. O night_____ di -

98

FAVORITE CANTATAS FOR ADVENT & CHRISTMAS

FESTIVAL OF CAROLS
Joseph M. Martin

Overflowing with tuneful praise, this cantata based on the traditional "Lessons and Carols" format, includes over 20 classic carols along with new seasonal selections. A full line of support products is available

35006579 SATB..$8.95

A SONG IS BORN
A CANTATA FOR CHRISTMAS
Douglas Nolan

Especially designed to enable quick and easy learning, this celebrative cantata is an ideal choice for churches with limited rehearsal times. Additional support products are available.

35000098 2-Part/SAB.................$7.95

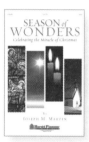

SEASON OF WONDERS
CELEBRATING THE MIRACLE OF CHRISTMAS
Joseph M. Martin

From the inspired pen of Joseph Martin comes a sacred work that will truly warm the hearts of all who hear it. Filled with classic carols as well as newly composed anthems, this hopeful work is both familiar and fresh, drawing the congregation close with brilliant orchestrations and poetic narrations. A full line of support products is available to help enable churches of every size to enjoy this outstanding seasonal offering.

35019290 SATB..$7.95

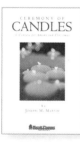

CEREMONY OF CANDLES
A CANTATA FOR ADVENT AND CHRISTMAS
Joseph M. Martin

From Joseph Martin comes a cantata that is filled with the wonder and light of Christmas. This imaginative new work uses carols and candlelight to embody the hope of Christ. Featuring orchestration by Brant Adams and narration by Pamela Stewart, this cantata empowers a director with many creative performance and programming options. Carols featured include: *In the Bleak Midwinter* • *Silent Night* • *O Come Little Children* • *What Child is This?* • *O Little Town of Bethlehem* • and many others.

35003163 SATB..$7.95

JOURNEY TO THE LIGHT
A CELEBRATION OF ADVENT
Don Besig/Nancy Price

Assembled from some of their best-selling anthems, this helpful collection is a splendid resource for your seasonal programming. Whether performed individually or as a mini-cantata, your choir will resonate with the simple messages of hope, peace, love and joy! This compilation can accompany your candle lighting each week to help create precious moments of reflection as you experience the journey of Christmas.

35011669 SATB..$7.95

THE WINTER ROSE
Joseph M. Martin

The Winter Rose incorporates both traditional carols and newly composed anthems that visit the timeless Christmas story with fresh insight. Through use of music, narration and simple symbolism, the cantata presents the life of Christ from prophecy to passion. The orchestrations effectively capture the essence of Joseph Martin's well-crafted piano writing, fully expressing the color and beauty of this musical tableau.

35025986 SATB..$7.95

ONCE UPON A NIGHT
Pepper Choplin

Written as a prequel to Pepper Choplin's best-selling Easter work, *Once Upon a Tree*, this new cantata follows closely the first two chapters of Luke. As the narrator, Luke leads worshippers through the story as he writes and reflects on the power and significance of the events. From the struggle and unbelief of Zechariah to the innocent faith of Mary, from the exuberance of the shepherds to the quiet joy of Simeon, Luke reveals the real human emotions of the story. The music is dramatic and is enriched with the masterful orchestrations of Brant Adams.

35016159 SATB..$7.95

www.shawneepress.com

Shawnee Press

Prices, contents, and availability
subject to change without notice.